Fountains of Fire

The story of
Auckland's volcanoes

By Geoffrey J. Cox

COLLINS
NEW ZEALAND

Acknowledgements

Information on Auckland's volcanoes is scattered not only amongst a number of sometimes obscure publications, but also through the minds of the region's vulcanologists. The production of this book would have been impossible without the help and guidance of Professor Manfred P. Hochstein, of the Geothermal Institute, University of Auckland, and the advice of Dr Les O. Kermode, of the DSIR Geological Survey. My sincere thanks to them both.

First published 1989

William Collins Publishers Ltd
P.O. Box 1, Auckland

Copyright © 1989 Geoffrey J. Cox

ISBN 0 00 217684 X

Typeset by Typeset Graphics Ltd, Auckland
Printed by Kings Time Printing Press Ltd,
Hong Kong

Contents

Introduction		1
1.	**What is a volcano?**	
	The origin of volcanoes; the eruption; Auckland's volcanoes	2
2.	**The time of the Auckland volcanoes**	6
3.	**The first eruptions**	
	Central Auckland; North Shore; West Auckland; South Auckland; One Tree Hill	8
4.	**The later eruptions**	
	Mount Mangere; Three Kings; Mount Smart; Mount Eden; Mount Wellington	18
5.	**The last eruption?**	
	Rangitoto; the volcanoes today; the future	24
Map of the remaining volcanoes of Auckland		28

For my father

Introduction

There is something a little odd about Auckland; every Aucklander must be aware of it, and even visitors would have to be remarkably unobservant not to notice it: the city is liberally scattered with volcanoes. Rangitoto, guarding the entrance to the Waitemata Harbour, is hard to miss — indeed, to be in sight of it could almost be taken as a definition of being in Auckland — but there are volcanoes all over the place. Climb to the top of any one of them and the chances are you will be able to pick out at least half a dozen others. In fact, there are far more than that — 48 to be precise, while in between them are about 75 square kilometres of lava flows that cover a fair portion of the Auckland isthmus. Rangitoto alone has 23 square kilometres of lava flow.

Not all Auckland's volcanoes are hills with craters at the top. Some, in fact, have been totally quarried away, while others never were more than large holes in the ground. It has taken 60,000 years to put them all here, but the most recent addition is only a few hundred years old and we can with complete confidence expect new volcanoes in the future. Fortunately, or unfortunately depending on how keen you are to add some very unusual photographs to the family album, the next eruption is probably a few centuries, or even millennia, away.

Why so many volcanoes, and why so small? And what was it like when they erupted? It is difficult, looking at today's picturesque, grass-covered hills, to believe, let alone imagine, that these gently sloping cones were once great slag-heaps of hot scoria, belching grey ash into the heavens while molten lava fountained in their craters and snaked away across the surrounding landscape. Sitting on their summits, far above the roar and bustle of the city, it is strange to think that once a far mightier roar came from these very summits. It was out of the desire to make this unbelievable past a little more real that this book was born.

1. What is a volcano?

Put simply, a volcano marks the point where molten rock from deep within the earth has reached the surface. Most volcanoes are not scattered at random over the earth but occur in chains, often extending for thousands of kilometres. This is no accident: very special conditions are required for the creation of volcanoes.

The origin of volcanoes

The surface of the earth is broken into about a dozen vast, slowly moving plates, each about 100 km thick, which together make up what is called the lithosphere. Resting on top of the lithosphere are the continents, which are about 35 km thick, while the lithosphere itself 'floats' on the asthenosphere. This 200 km-thick layer is so hot (about 1300-1400°C) that the rock is close to its melting point (indeed, it would melt if the pressure were less) and is capable of plastic flow.

One type of volcanism occurs where two plates collide. Normally, one plate slides beneath the other, plunging into the asthenosphere. Since the rocks at the top of the lithosphere melt at a lower temperature than those deeper down, they do so, normally at a depth of about 150 km, forming *magma,* which 'squirts' up cracks created by the collision in the over-riding plate to form *andesitic* volcanoes. The upper plate often carries a continent (which never sinks), so such volcanoes frequently occur along the edges of a land mass. The Andes in South America are the archetypal example, but andesitic volcanism also occurs in New Zealand where the Pacific plate is in collision with the Australian-Indian plate, splitting the New Zealand continent which happens to straddle the boundary. The volcanoes of the central North Island and White Island are andesitic volcanoes.

Occasionally, asthenosphere material rises with the magma from the newly-melted lithosphere. The continental crust itself may then melt at a depth of only 10 km or so. Large amounts of gas can be produced and when the gas pressure exceeds the confining pressure of the rock above, there is a cataclysmic, *rhyolitic* eruption. This is what happened at Lake Taupo in about 180 AD. Most of the North Island was covered in several metres of debris, and so much ash was thrown into the upper atmosphere that the ancient Chinese were moved to comment on the unusually red sunsets.

Asthenospheric rock can rise less destructively where two plates are being pulled slowly apart. As the pressure falls, the rock melts and the lighter portion rises through the lithosphere to spew out on the surface. Most large-scale melting of asthenosphere rocks occurs at the centre of oceans where the resulting volcanoes give rise to the mid-ocean ridges and, occasionally, islands such as Iceland.

Magma from the asthenosphere can, however, rise to the surface in the centre of plates. This may happen where a plate is under tension, causing deep cracks to develop, as is the case in East Africa. It also occurs over a 'hot spot' in the asthenosphere, such as exists below the Hawaiian Islands.

The eruption

Volcanic eruptions vary from gentle to violent, depending on the amount of gas in the magma. This gas consists not only of dissolved gases that separate out as the pressure falls, but also of steam, often derived from water-saturated layers encountered by the ascending molten rock. The gases cause the magma to froth and, upon reaching the surface, the frothy, gas-rich portion is ejected as *ash, lapilli* or *scoria,* while the rather gas-free portion flows out as *lava.* The violence of the eruption thus depends on how far the separation of gas from rock has proceeded, with poorly-separated eruptions being the more violent.

High steam pressure in shallow surface layers can ensure that a new volcano starts with a bang, for superheated steam can throw up a considerable quantity of rock (a *phreatic* explosion), creating a deep crater rimmed by a raised lip of ejected, non-volcanic rock called *tuff.*

The most violent explosions of all, however, occur when large quantities of crustal rock melt, such as happened at Lake Taupo.

With these factors influencing the nature of the eruption, it is possible to divide the world's volcanoes into five basic types, only one of which, the mildest — yet, paradoxically, the most spectacular — need concern us here. It is called the *Hawaiian* eruption and in it lava fountains from one or more vents — the appropriately named fire fountains — building scoria cones about those vents and, if there is sufficient lava, forming lava flows.

Once free of the crater, the 'runnyness' of the lava is determined by its temperature and the amount of gas in it. A hot lava, rich in gas, will flow readily and cover large distances, travelling at speeds of up to 50 km per hour. A thin, smooth skin forms upon its surface within which the lava flows as if in an insulating tube. Such flows cool to a rippled, 'ropey' textured rock known by its Hawaiian name of *pahoehoe*.

Gas-poor flows are more viscous. They travel slowly — often only a few kilometres per hour — with a rough, broken surface of cooled rock. They are known by the Hawaiian name of *aa* — probably a reference to the sounds made by anyone attempting to cross a hardened flow in bare feet!

Very viscous, rhyolitic lava may not flow at all, but simply squeeze up into a growing mound which, being very hot, stretches to accommodate it. Mount Ngongotaha near Rotorua is an example of such a volcano.

Auckland's volcanoes

Auckland's volcanoes are probably the result of a small hot spot formed where a plate is under tension. Every now and then, a bubble of asthenosphere magma rises through the solid rock of the lithosphere towards the surface. It may travel surprisingly quickly, making the entire trip in only a few weeks.

As it nears the surface, the reduction in pressure causes gases dissolved in the magma to separate out, and it may also encounter ground water which flashes to steam. In either event, the high pressures generated cause an explosion and a new Auckland volcano is born.

What happens next depends on the size of the bubble. A small bubble (only a few hundred tonnes of magma) may totally expend itself in this one explosion, or perhaps in several explosions in quick succession, leaving an explosion crater as its only legacy. A larger bubble will still have energy left, and will go on to build scoria cones and maybe produce lava flows. Many Auckland volcanoes produced very runny pahoehoe flows, but aa flows can be found too, especially on Rangitoto.

With the exhaustion of the bubble, most Auckland volcanoes became extinct, although it is possible that the larger ones such as One Tree Hill and Rangitoto tapped a succession of bubbles over several centuries. Even here, however, the bubbles eventually stopped coming. Since, unlike other volcanoes, there is no large magma reservoir below them, Auckland volcanoes will not erupt again. One day, however, somewhere near by, another bubble will approach the surface and the cycle will be repeated.

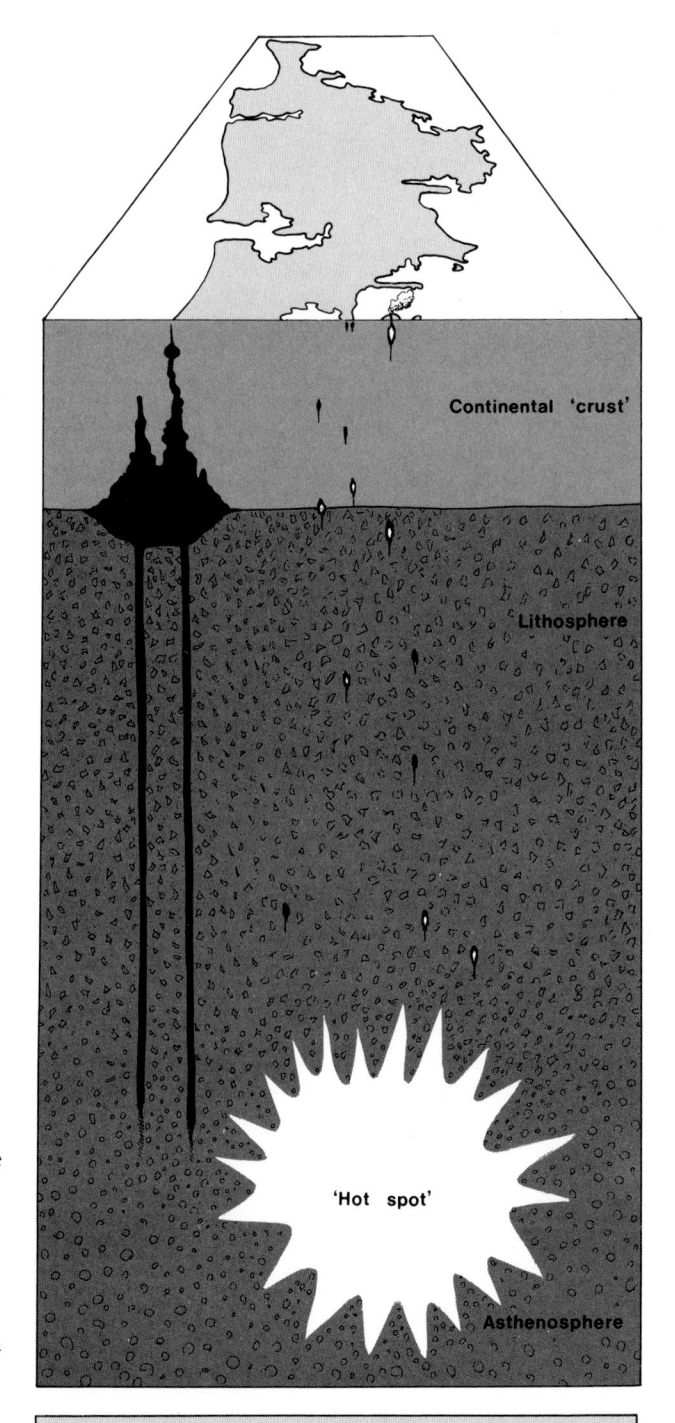

A cross-section through the first 150 km or so of earth below Auckland at the time of the eruption of Rangitoto. The volcano is visible towards the centre, feeding off a magma bubble, while another rises towards the volcano through the upper lithosphere. Immediately to the west (left) of Rangitoto are the two dead magma bubbles of North Head and Mount Victoria, while further to the west are the long-extinct magma reservoirs and chambers of the andesitic Waitakere volcanoes.

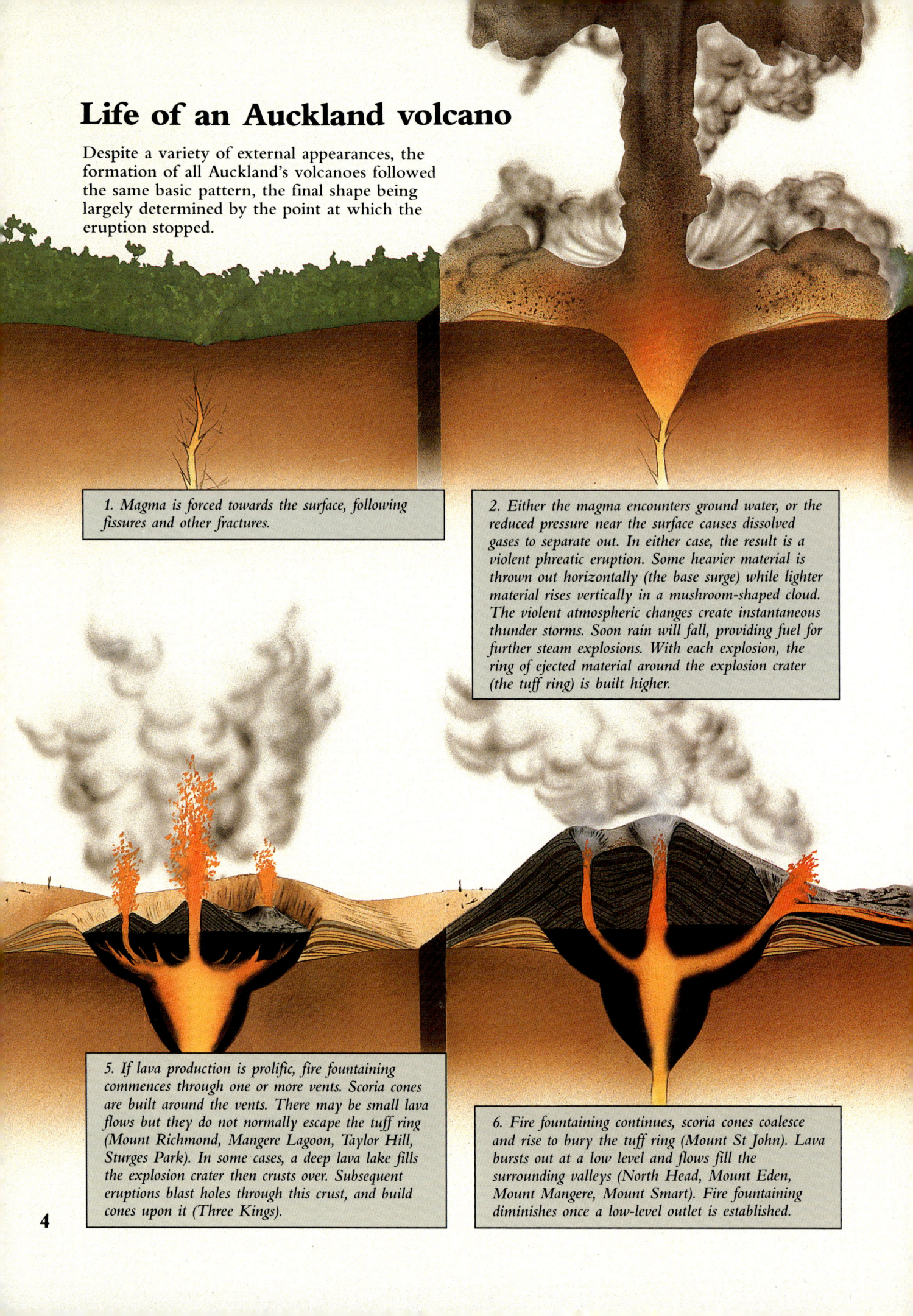

Life of an Auckland volcano

Despite a variety of external appearances, the formation of all Auckland's volcanoes followed the same basic pattern, the final shape being largely determined by the point at which the eruption stopped.

1. Magma is forced towards the surface, following fissures and other fractures.

2. Either the magma encounters ground water, or the reduced pressure near the surface causes dissolved gases to separate out. In either case, the result is a violent phreatic eruption. Some heavier material is thrown out horizontally (the base surge) while lighter material rises vertically in a mushroom-shaped cloud. The violent atmospheric changes create instantaneous thunder storms. Soon rain will fall, providing fuel for further steam explosions. With each explosion, the ring of ejected material around the explosion crater (the tuff ring) is built higher.

5. If lava production is prolific, fire fountaining commences through one or more vents. Scoria cones are built around the vents. There may be small lava flows but they do not normally escape the tuff ring (Mount Richmond, Mangere Lagoon, Taylor Hill, Sturges Park). In some cases, a deep lava lake fills the explosion crater then crusts over. Subsequent eruptions blast holes through this crust, and build cones upon it (Three Kings).

6. Fire fountaining continues, scoria cones coalesce and rise to bury the tuff ring (Mount St John). Lava bursts out at a low level and flows fill the surrounding valleys (North Head, Mount Eden, Mount Mangere, Mount Smart). Fire fountaining diminishes once a low-level outlet is established.

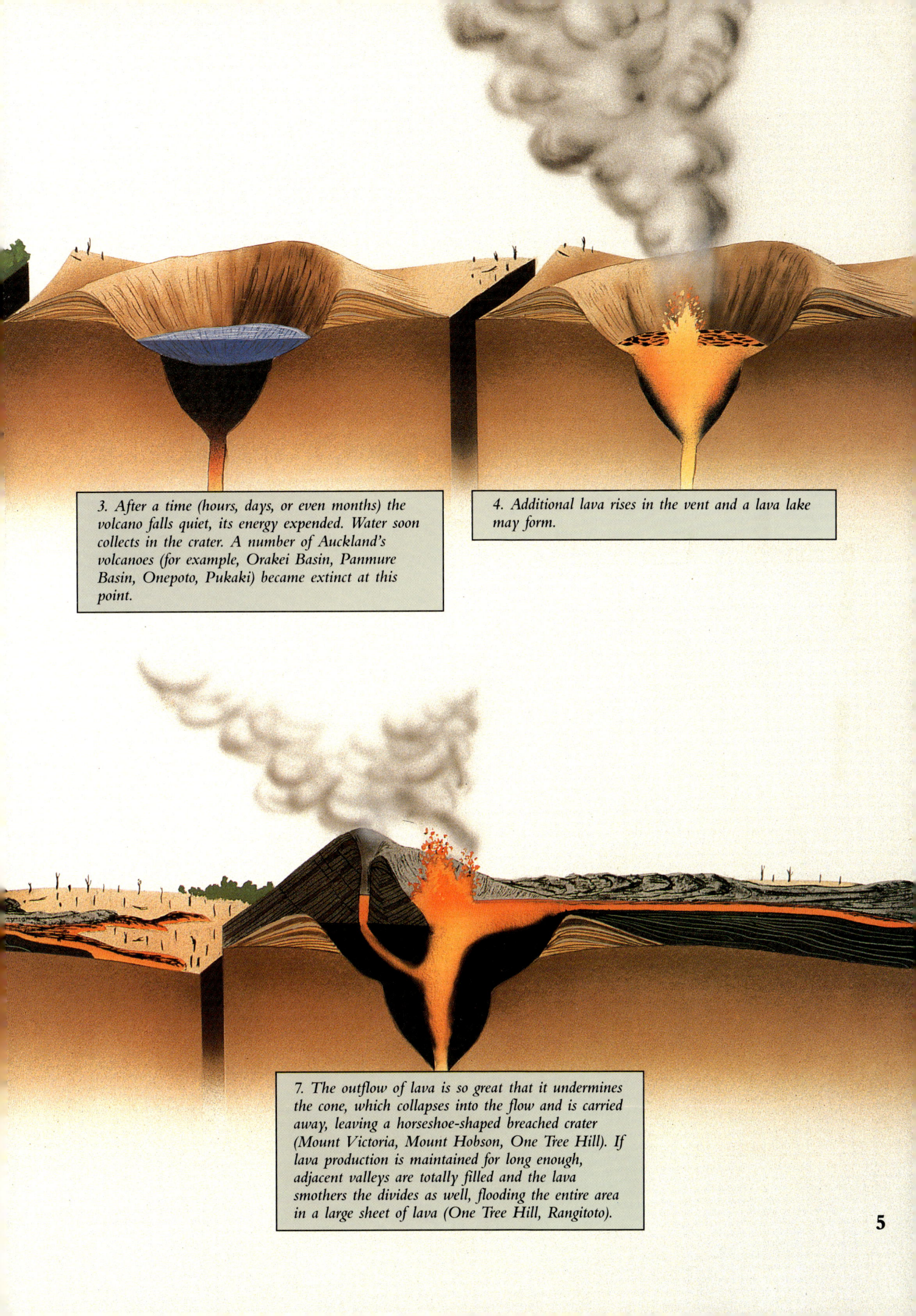

3. After a time (hours, days, or even months) the volcano falls quiet, its energy expended. Water soon collects in the crater. A number of Auckland's volcanoes (for example, Orakei Basin, Panmure Basin, Onepoto, Pukaki) became extinct at this point.

4. Additional lava rises in the vent and a lava lake may form.

7. The outflow of lava is so great that it undermines the cone, which collapses into the flow and is carried away, leaving a horseshoe-shaped breached crater (Mount Victoria, Mount Hobson, One Tree Hill). If lava production is maintained for long enough, adjacent valleys are totally filled and the lava smothers the divides as well, flooding the entire area in a large sheet of lava (One Tree Hill, Rangitoto).

2. The time of the Auckland volcanoes

This planet generally seems a very stable place, but when viewed on a time scale of thousands or millions of years it can be seen to be in a constant state of flux. We have already noted that the lithosphere plates, and the continents that ride upon them, are in constant slow motion. Superimposed upon this are other changes — less permanent, perhaps, but no less traumatic. In the past few million years, the most significant of these have been the great Ice Ages.

Starting 2,500,000 years ago, temperatures have fallen four times and ice sheets have expanded outwards from the poles and high mountains to cover vast areas of the earth. On each occasion, the amount of water locked up in these sheets was so great that sea levels fell by well over 100 metres. Between each Ice Age came a period when temperatures were as warm or warmer than they are today, and sea levels were above their present level. The last Ice Age began about 100,000 years ago, and was at its peak when volcanic activity began in Auckland.

In New Zealand, sea level fell from a height of 12 to 20 metres above the present level to about 120 metres below. The Manukau and Waitemata harbours became wide, forested valleys as the coastline retreated to beyond the mouth of the Manukau in the west and to beyond Great Barrier Island in the east.

At the same time, it was much colder than it is today. Most of the South Island and much of the North were covered in alpine or subalpine grassland or permanent ice. Only in low-lying areas around the coast and in the north did substantial areas of forest remain. Surprisingly, that in the Auckland region appears to have been little different from that remaining in northern New Zealand today.

The ice finally began to melt in New Zealand about 14,000 years ago — about 4,000 years earlier than in many parts of the world. By about 10,000 years ago, the sea level in this country had risen to about 75 metres below the present level, and subsequently rose at a rate of about a metre a century until, between 5,500 and 4,000 years ago, it peaked at up to three metres above the present level. After that, it receded again, but evidence suggests that today it is rising once more.

Thus most of Auckland's volcanoes were born not into the present, almost subtropical, landscape of shallow harbours and scattered islands, but into a cold world of wide valleys and low hills. While we do not know with any certainty when most of the volcanoes erupted, we do know that, with the exception of Rangitoto, lava flows that today run beneath the sea originally flowed on dry land, and volcanoes

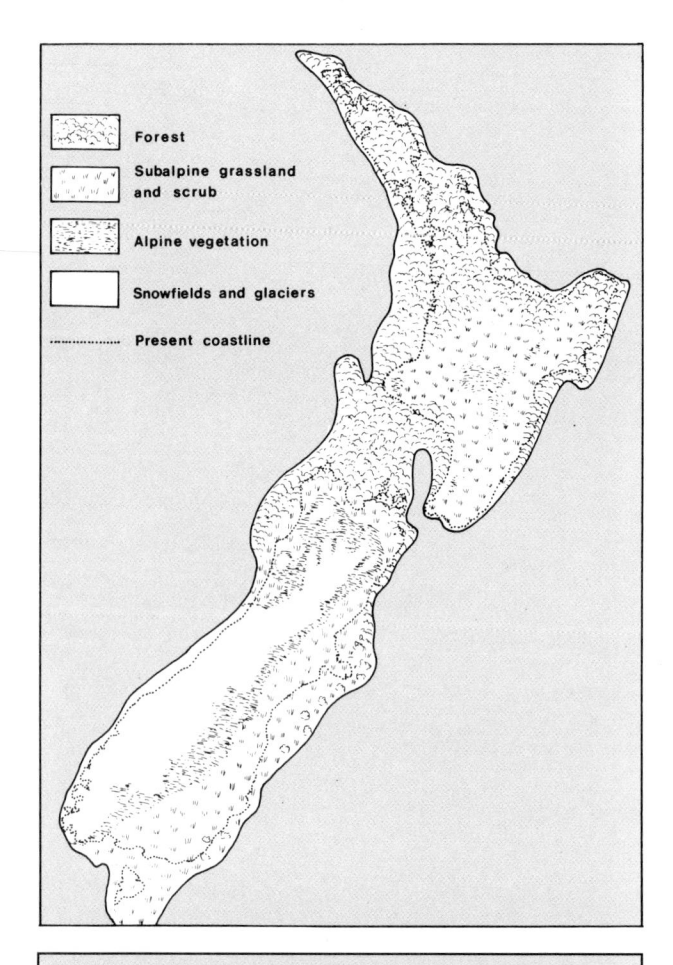

At the height of the last Ice Age the sea level was so low that New Zealand was a single island. Most of it was covered in alpine tussock grass, and extensive sheets of permanent ice buried the high alpine areas. Only around the coast and in the north did forest survive. The dotted line indicates the coastline today.

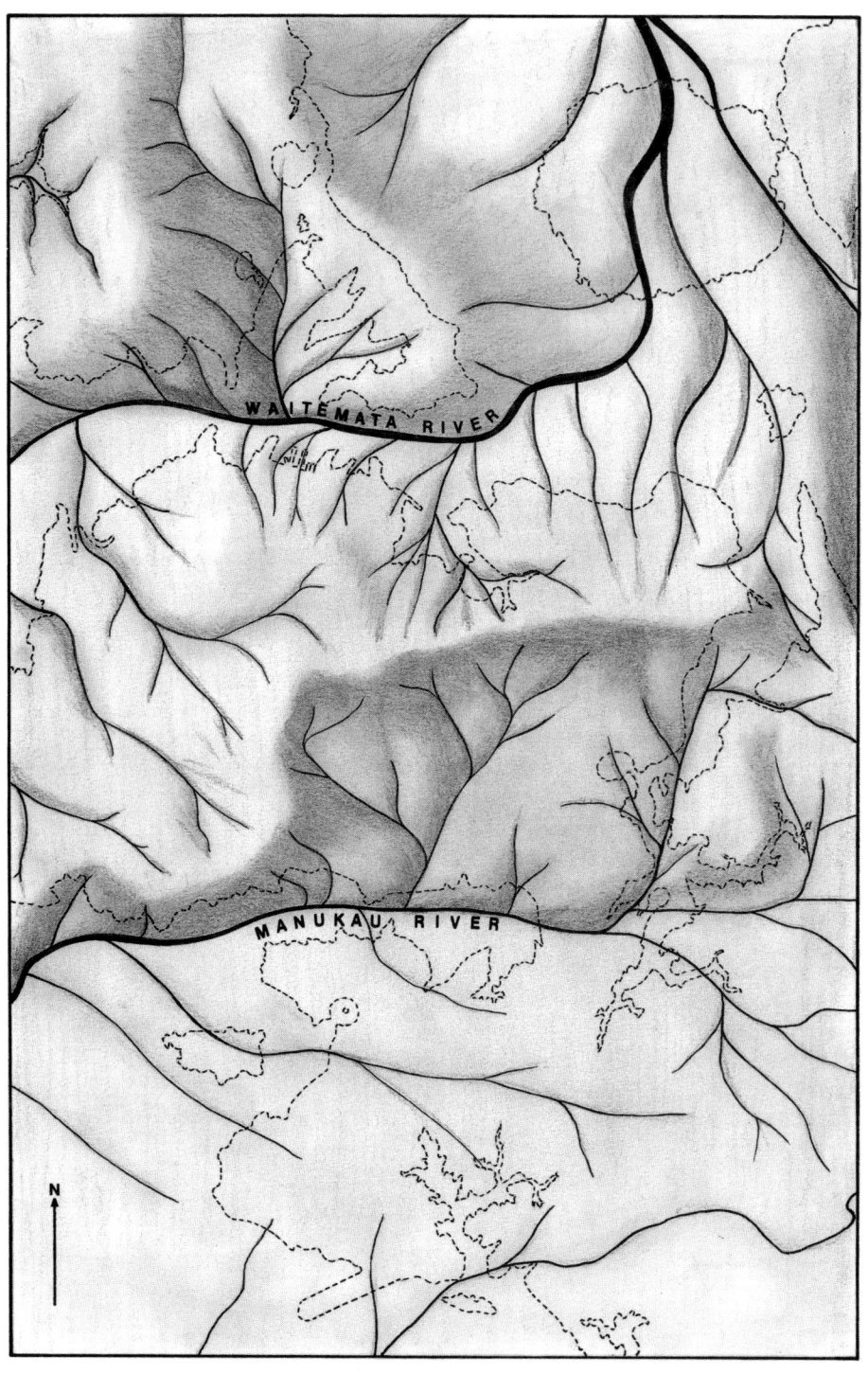

that today are islands, headlands or tidal lagoons did not encounter sea water when they erupted. During the 60,000 years of their history, they totally changed the Auckland landscape, blasting new depressions into the ground and filling old ones with their cones, tuff and flows. In places, the land we see today is virtually an inverted landscape, with peninsulas jutting where bays would have been, and hills rising where valleys once lay. In many ways and for many reasons, Auckland was a very different place when it all began.

At the start of the volcanic period, Auckland consisted of two wide river valleys separated by a low divide. The ancient Manukau and Waitemata rivers flowed down the centre of what are now the Manukau and Waitemata Harbours, fed by numerous streams from the surrounding country. To the south of the Manukau River was a wide plain, created by the blanket of ash that, for several thousand years by now, had been regularly deposited from the huge volcanoes of the Taupo volcanic zone. The dashed line indicates the coastline today.

3. The first eruptions
(60,000-18,000 years ago)

The vast forest is deep, dank and silent. Huge kauri trees tower 50 metres and more into the air, bursting through the forest canopy of rata and rimu, while on the forest floor, ferns and creepers create an almost impenetrable barrier. The only sounds to break the silence are the gurgle of the streams and the calls of birds. Innumerable birds — tuis, bellbirds, kakas, fantails, riflemen, stitchbirds and huias, to name but a few — flit through the forest, their calls mingling and echoing between the trees, while kiwis, wekas and moas stalk the floor below. This is a forest of birds.

It is cold. Winter grips the forest with an icy intensity, for this is the Ice Age. Not so very far to the south is a treeless waste of tussock grass that stretches almost unbroken to the southern tip of New Zealand. This northern forest is lucky to be here at all.

Overnight, the millennia-old peace of the land was disturbed by a series of earth tremors. Neither long nor strong, they have done no damage. Now, however, the grey light of dawn reveals a new phenomenon: high on the gently sloping side of a valley, steam emerges from the ground to drift off silently among the trees. As the morning advances, the intensity of the steam emission increases, undermining trees and creating cavities in the ground. Not far below the surface, magma is rising, encountering ground water that flashes to steam which must force its way to the open air. Suddenly, with a mighty roar, a great section of forest is hurled skywards.

A thick cloud of rocks and earth bursts out horizontally across the land, levelling trees in its path, while a mushroom-shaped cloud of lighter debris boils high into the air, creating an instantaneous thunderstorm. Soon rain begins to fall, but far from dousing the new volcano the water is turned to steam, leading to further explosions. Eventually, however, the initial force of the eruption is spent and a temporary peace returns to the land.

Now the full extent of the damage becomes apparent. Where once mature trees stood, there is a wide, circular crater some 300 metres across, rimmed with a layered pile of rubble and earth about 60 metres high. Within this wall, the crater floor slopes steeply downwards to a point at its centre where steam is rising from among the jumbled boulders.

Within hours, molten rock from beneath the earth begins to ooze to the surface through a number of outlets, slowly at first, but with increasing vigour until it is fountaining to heights of several hundred metres while cones of scoria build around each vent. The cones grow in size and merge into a single, complex mound with several craters that quickly starts to bury the encircling tuff ring. As night falls, the fountaining lava provides an awesome spectacle.

Before midnight, the lava has forced its way through the base of the cone and, overtopping the tuff ring, pours down into the valley, riding over the trunks of trees felled in the earlier explosions and on into the still-standing forest. Trees flame like torches as the molten rock engulfs them, and come crashing down to be absorbed into the flow. The stream in the valley bottom turns to steam as the lava reaches it and, for a while, water is replaced by lava as the flow follows the course of the stream bed. All night long the lava snakes downstream, fed by the rumbling volcano that dominates the skyline.

Over the next few days, many flows follow that first one down into the valley, until the original stream bed is buried under many metres of cooling rock. Eventually, the flows spill over the low divide into the neighbouring valley, filling that one in turn and creating a plateau of basalt in its place. The magma supply, however, is nearly exhausted. Slowly, the quantity of lava flowing from the vents diminishes and, finally, ceases all together.

Now only the central vent of the volcano is still active, but instead of a fire fountain it scatters ash into the sky. Every now and then the output dies away, sometimes for some hours as expelled material clogs the vent, only to be resumed when a violent explosion clears the blockage. For several days, ash showers down upon new lava flows and ancient forest alike, burying all in what will, in time, become a rich soil. Eventually, however, the ash eruption stops completely, and this time there is no reviving explosion.

Steam drifts lazily from the craters of the

new volcano. It will continue to do so for some years, while fumaroles will dot the surface of the lava flows for decades. But this volcano will never erupt again.

The above account, loosely based on what we know of the eruption of Mount Albert, gives an idea of how the eruption of one of the larger Auckland volcanoes may have proceeded. The duration of activity is the most variable aspect. Several weeks are implied in this account, but it could have continued intermittently for considerably longer or, on the other hand, have been completed in a matter of days.

It all began in what is today the heart of Auckland. A small volcano, centred near a valley bottom, began life explosively, showering the adjacent valley slope with a considerable quantity of tuff. Subsequently, a small cone was built that breached to the west, letting lava flood down the valley side and into the stream at the bottom. Here, a flow of considerable thickness was built, up-stream of which a lake and subsequently a swamp developed that remained until drained by Europeans 60,000 years later.

The stream valley is now Queen Street, the tuff-covered slope is Albert Park, and the volcano itself stood somewhere near the Magistrate's Court. The lava flow passed down Victoria Street to the intersection, then on downtown almost as far as Fort Street. Thus, while the backs of the buildings on the west side of Queen Street rest on non-volcanic rock, their fronts, and most of the buildings on the east side, stand upon this ancient flow — a fact that has greatly complicated the building of Auckland.

The scene, depicting the final stages of the eruption, is viewed from Victoria Street west of Queen Street. New lava floods over older flows, passing under what will one day be the Victoria Street car park, while the dammed stream (hidden behind the brow of the hill) sends up a cloud of steam as it meets the molten rock.

The picture at left depicts the same view as it appears today.

Central Auckland eruptions

The eruption of Auckland's first volcano was probably even briefer. Sixty thousand years or more ago, on a site now occupied by the Magistrate's Court and the corner of Albert Park, a volcano erupted and filled the adjacent valley (Queen Street) with its lava flow. At about the same time, another volcano was creating havoc in what is now the Domain. A small lava flow slipped round the future site of Auckland Hospital, which today stands on one edge of the tuff ring. The museum stands on the other, and the glasshouses upon the remains of a small scoria cone that rose in the centre.

North Shore eruptions

In the north of Auckland, activity also began explosively, perhaps 40,000 years ago, with a series of phreatic eruptions that created the explosion craters of Onepoto, Tank Farm and Pupuke. Of these, Pupuke was the most complex, with a number of explosions from different centres. Some scoria cones were built and lava flows produced, especially along what is now the seaward edge (where they saved the crater from becoming another tidal lagoon, preserving it as a fresh water lake instead). However, the eruption turned explosive again in its final stages, destroying the cones and creating the large, unevenly-shaped crater we see today.

A much smaller explosion crater lies, partly buried and partly destroyed by sea, beneath North Head which, together with Mount Cambria (now quarried away) and Mount Victoria, are also thought to have erupted during this early period.

West Auckland eruptions

The first prolific lava producer and the largest cone at the time was Mount Albert, which erupted more than 30,000 years ago. The present cone bears little resemblance to the original for extensive quarrying has removed at least the top 15 metres and the three craters have been widened to hold playing fields. Some time later, Mount Roskill erupted and sent lava flowing down the same valley as Mount Albert so that today the stream within it flows round the western edge of both flows. In contrast to its neighbour, Mount Roskill has been little affected by quarrying. Its rather dumpy cone with its shallow twin craters (now two car parks) and even a remnant of its tuff ring (in the Akarana Golf Course) remain intact today.

South Auckland eruptions

Fifteen kilometres to the south east, the volcanoes of the Ihumatao, Papatoetoe and Wiri regions, the most southerly volcanoes in the Auckland area, erupted. Activity at Papatoetoe was largely explosive, although events were more complex at Crater Hill. Here a lava lake for a while filled the crater, followed by the rise of a small scoria cone. Then the still-molten lava drained back into the vent and the solidified crust collapsed into the crater, leaving a 'high-water mark' rim of solid lava round the edge. Today, Crater Hill is the site of a quarry, but the almost perfect circle of nearby Pukaki remains intact as one of the best examples of an explosion crater in Auckland.

The Ihumatao group of volcanoes are among the few which have been well dated. This is normally possible only when charred wood suitable for Carbon 14 dating is found beneath flows or tuff, as is the case here where an age of 29,000 years is indicated. The Wiri volcanoes, dated by the same method, are about 1,000 years younger. Today all these volcanoes have been badly damaged, or even totally destroyed, by quarrying.

The first few minutes of life of the volcano that was later to be known by the prosaic name of Tank Farm were undoubtedly its most spectacular. With an ear-splitting explosion, a huge eruption cloud is hurled skywards, while heavier material rolls out sideways — the 'base surge'. With many Auckland volcanoes such an explosion was but the start of the eruption sequence, but at Tank Farm, as at the neighbouring Onepoto Basin, it is all there was. The base surge formed the foundations of the tuff ring and the lighter material from the mushroom cloud settled upon it. A few more explosions may have repeated the sequence, but it was soon all over. Today, these two volcanoes lie right next to the motorway, only a kilometre or so north of the Harbour Bridge, yet many who pass them daily are unaware of their existence.

The scene is viewed from what is today Marine Terrace in Bayswater; then it was the high land on the far side of a thickly forested valley. When excavating spoil for the harbour bridge approach, the evidence for this forest was found in the form of casts of huge trees that had been buried in the Onepoto tuff — trees with trunks up to five metres in diameter that rose 18 metres to the first branch. Unfortunately, the wood had long since decayed, so Carbon 14 dating of these eruptions has not been possible.

The photograph is of Lake Pupuke, Auckland's largest explosion crater, with Rangitoto in the background. The view is from the top floor of North Shore Hospital.

It seems that most of the remaining volcanoes of South Auckland were created at an early date in eruptions that typically petered out not long after the initial explosion. Thus we see a few simple explosion craters such as the Panmure Basin and Pukekiwiriki, and several 'castle and moat' volcanoes with explosion craters surrounding one or more little cones. Two neighbouring volcanoes, Sturges Park and Mount Richmond, represent the extremes of such volcanoes. At the former site, the explosion crater surrounds a single, centrally-located cone while at the latter, fire fountaining from at least seven vents produced a cluster of little cones, the largest of which just buried one edge of the tuff ring. This volcano produced little lava, but the nearby McLennan Hills, which date from the same time, were prolific lava producers, exuding a wide flow that dammed the upper reaches of the Manukau River.

One Tree Hill eruption

And then, in the midst of all these fairly small eruptions, rose Auckland's first giant: One Tree Hill. Copious lava was produced from a great variety of vents, several of which were no doubt buried under the growing volcano. The present cone lies on a bed of lava 60 to 80 metres thick. In its final stages three vast craters were active, two of which were breached to produce the final flows while the third remained intact near the present summit.

Flows ran as far north as the edge of the Domain, and south almost to the Manukau River. Valleys were filled and ridges smothered as more than half a cubic kilometre of lava was produced. There is even a possibility that a small, earlier volcano was totally buried. The eruption has recently been dated — using a photoluminescent technique originally developed to date pottery in archaeological digs — to about 18,000 years ago. It was to be more than 17,000 years before Auckland again saw lava production on such a lavish scale.

Fire fountaining provides a spectacular spot of colour on a grey day approximately 40,000 years ago. The volcano in eruption is North Head, viewed from what is today the Tamaki Drive. To the right of the cone, an ash shower obliterates the lower reaches of the Waitemata River valley. To the left, the recently-formed cones of Mount Cambria and Mount Victoria stand stark and bare, steam still drifting from the crater of the latter. Mount Victoria produced a small flow which undermined the cone to the south and breached the crater. The collapsed remnant of the cone was carried for several hundred metres by the lava before coming to rest on what would one day be the Devonport foreshore. Early settlers named this little hill (barely 15 metres from its base to summit) 'Duders' and, until recently, it has been incorrectly considered to be a cone in its own right. Like Mount Cambria, it has long since been quarried away.

13

The sudden resumption of activity after a period of quiescence startles moas (Dinornis giganteus) feeding on land cleared by earlier eruptions of the proto One Tree Hill. Like Mount Eden, but unlike most of the other Auckland volcanoes, activity at One Tree Hill was apparently spread over some years, with periods of inactivity between eruptions long enough for vegetation to grow on the old lava flows. The open land may have attracted the giant moas, which were then surprised, and often trapped, by the renewed volcanic activity. At the stage of its life depicted here, One Tree Hill bears no relationship to its final form. The picture at right shows One Tree Hill today, from the south.

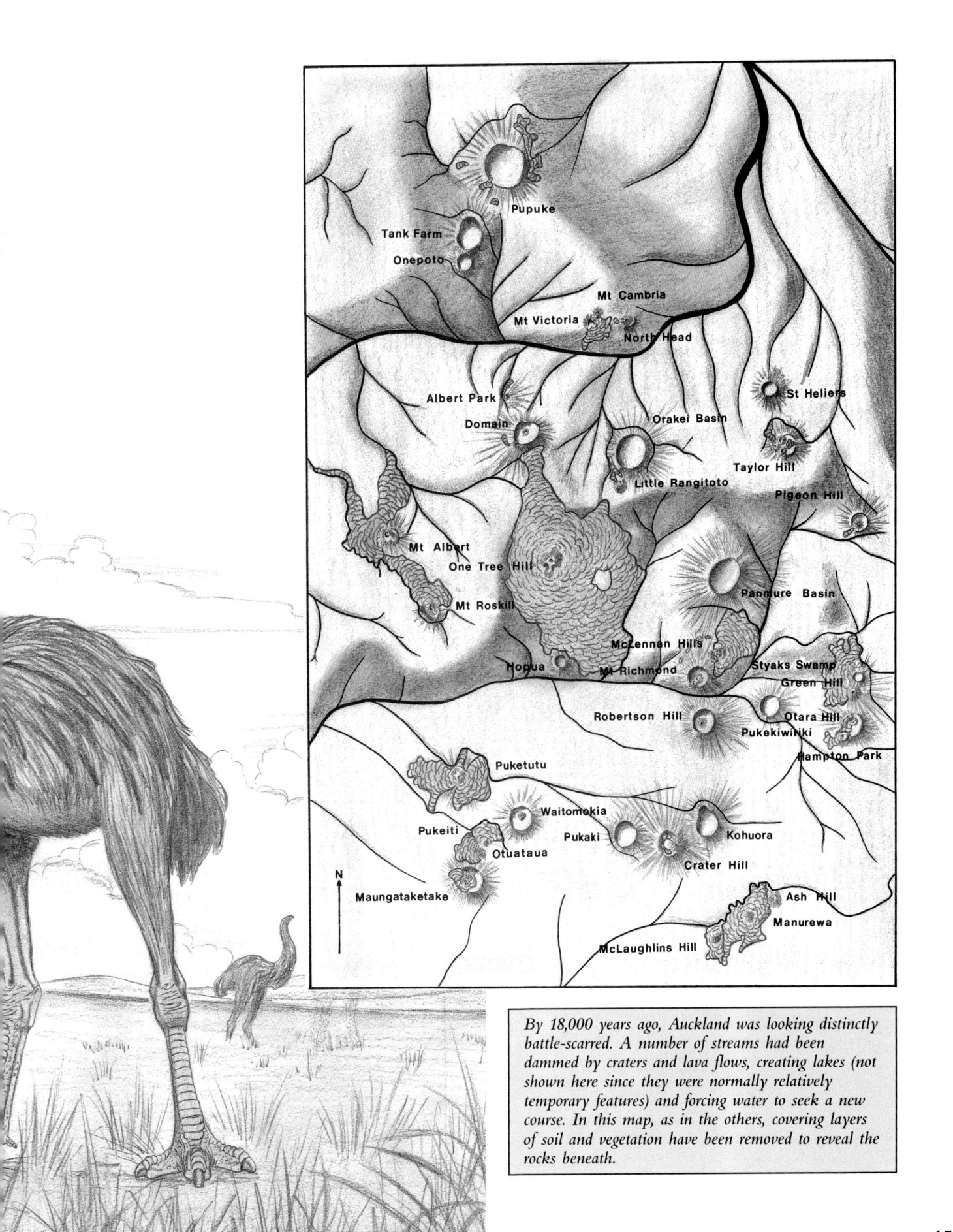

By 18,000 years ago, Auckland was looking distinctly battle-scarred. A number of streams had been dammed by craters and lava flows, creating lakes (not shown here since they were normally relatively temporary features) and forcing water to seek a new course. In this map, as in the others, covering layers of soil and vegetation have been removed to reveal the rocks beneath.

15

4. The later eruptions
(18,000-9,000 years ago)

The eruption of One Tree Hill seems to have heralded a more active phase in Auckland's volcanic history. The next 9,000 years saw the creation of many of the area's larger volcanoes and most of the more substantial lava flows.

Mount Mangere eruption
Mount Mangere erupted within a few hundred years of One Tree Hill. Its fluid lava flowed in a thin sheet down into the adjacent Manukau River valley, forcing the river to divert round the northern edge of the flow. Thousands of years later, the fact that this flow was so thin had unexpected repercussions. The builders of the first Mangere bridge, digging down through the mud of the Manukau Harbour, discovered basalt and, no doubt assuming that, like so many other Auckland flows, it would be of considerable thickness, fixed the foundations of the bridge upon it. Alas, it was barely a metre thick and soon broke under the weight, resulting in the curiously hump-backed structure that, for many years, was the main route to Auckland Airport from the north. Today it has been superseded, but still remains to the west of the new bridge as an unexpected tribute to the unpredictability of volcanoes!

Hours after the eruption that created it, steam drifting from the many eruption centres of Mount Mangere provide eloquent testimony of the complexity of its history. Even today, 18,300 years later, several fire pits are distinguishable in the huge main crater, and other eruption centres created a deep crater to the right in this view, and a wide breached crater (now a playing field) in front. At about the same time, a violent explosion just to the south-west created the Mangere Lagoon — the major source of steam in this picture.

Towards the end of the eruption, after fire fountaining had finished in the main crater, there was a rise in pressure again in a central fire pit. A plug of semi-hardened lava (called a tholoid) was pushed upwards many metres before, finally, the volcano gave up the struggle or possibly found an alternative exit in the rim to the north-east. The tholoid, however, remains today and, to the uninitiated, looks not unlike a miniature cone within the crater.

Lava from Mount Mangere covered a wide area in almost every direction and was subsequently buried below a thick layer of ash that accounts for the utter desolation of this scene.

The newly-formed volcano is viewed from what was than a point further up the Manukau River valley; today it is the northern shore of the suburb of Favona (picture, left). The high point on the crater rim survived until the arrival of the Europeans, but is gone today.

Three Kings eruption

One Tree Hill may have provided Auckland with its most effusive eruption for many millennia, but for sheer explosive force only one other volcano has ever come close to Three Kings. Looking at the battered, quarry-scarred remnant of the volcano today, it is hard to believe that Three Kings erupted with a force which, should it happen now, would shatter every window in central Auckland. One Tree Hill's lava flows were so deeply buried in tuff from the explosion that, to this day, we are unsure of their true extent.

Mount Smart eruption

Up through the edge of the lava flows of One Tree Hill came Mount Smart, its own flows covering some of those of the earlier eruption. Although the lava fields are not extensive, they are thick, and those to the south bear evidence of a complex history. It would appear that here, for a while, the flow was dammed. When the lava finally found an escape route into the Manukau River valley, the result was a four-metre drop in the liquid level. The crust of the impounded flow collapsed, and the uneven surface of the land in this area remains even today as a reminder of that time.

Mount Smart itself was a squat cone that nevertheless rose some 60 metres above its base to a height of 87 metres above modern sea level — a fact that is hard to credit today when quarrying and subsequent redevelopment have turned it into a major sports stadium.

View to the west from the summit of Mount Roskill about 12,000 years ago: Mount Eden in eruption. The eruption is seen as it enters its last stages. Fire fountaining has commenced at the most westerly of the three craters that make up the cone, but the final outpourings of lava, which will build up a high plateau about the base of the volcano, have yet to occur. The numerous cones to the right of Mount Eden in fact represent only three volcanoes. The more distant cones to the left and right are Mount St John and One Tree Hill respectively, while the five in the centre are the Three Kings complex (the three largest of which gave rise to the name). The tuff crater of this volcano extends from just to the left of the rata tree in the foreground to immediately to the right of Mount St John, with the high point of the eastern rim just visible between the cones. Today, all save this and the second cone from the left have been totally destroyed by quarrying. All the cones other than Mount Eden appear higher than they do today due to their thick covering of mature forest. The picture at right is today's view from the same perspective.

Mount Eden eruption

About 12,000 years ago came a volcano to rival One Tree Hill in the size of its cone, at least, if not of its flows: Mount Eden. Like One Tree Hill this volcano apparently erupted in several phases. A deep well, sunk into the flows near the base of the cone, found several sheets of lava interspersed with beds of scoria and of swamp-laid silts with plant remains that could have been deposited only during periods of quiet.

Hemmed in on most sides by older flows and tuff deposits, the flows of Mount Eden did not spread far, but did reach a considerable depth. The diggers of the well gave up at 60 metres, having still not reached the non-volcanic rock beneath.

Just to the south of Mount Eden there was, until the start of this century, a curious little volcano called Te Pouhawaiki. Very low, yet with a surprisingly large crater, it looked much as though it was the summit of a bigger cone buried in its neighbour's flow, although it could equally have been a later addition that presumably exhausted itself punching a hole through that mass of basalt. At all events, it proved far too small to survive the ravages of the European settlers and is totally destroyed today.

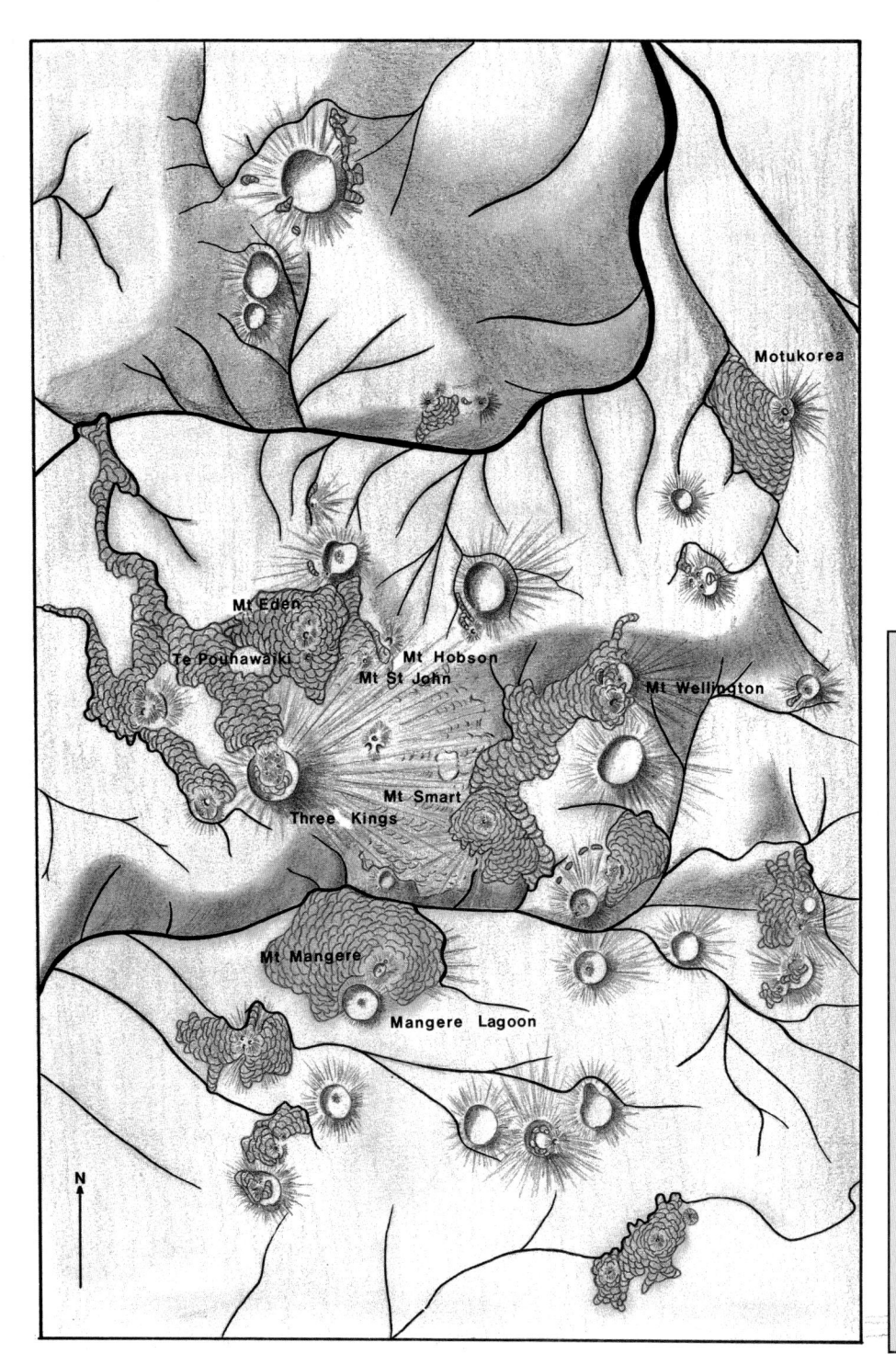

Looking more like some bizarre lunar landscape than the future site of a major city, Auckland 9,000 years ago was a confused mass of explosion craters, scoria cones and lava flows. Both the Waitemata and Manukau Rivers had been diverted by lava flows, and several smaller streams had had their entire valleys totally obliterated. In some instances, the streams were able to return to their original course after the eruption, flowing along cracks created in the lava as it cooled. When these streams finally surfaced, they formed substantial springs such as Western Springs, once the water supply for much of the city.

Mount Wellington eruption

A little over 9,000 years ago came another volcanic giant (in Auckland terms). Indeed, ultimately it would build the largest scoria cone to date.

The eruption commenced in the traditional manner with the creation of an explosion crater, the rise of lava, then fire fountaining from a couple of vents that built a small, twin-cratered scoria hill. Activity died down and, perhaps for as long as a century, all was quiet. Then pressure rose again. By now, however, the entire floor of the crater was sealed by a great plate of solid basalt that proved impervious to the rising magma. Instead, the magma forced a way round the side of this shield, possibly actually tilting it in the process, to burst out at the rim of the tuff ring. This time, fire fountaining was long and vigorous and the lava flows copious. The result was Mount Wellington, the 134 metre-high cone of which has a volume of more than 8,000,000 cubic metres. The small, earlier cone was Purchas Hill, which has now been quarried away.

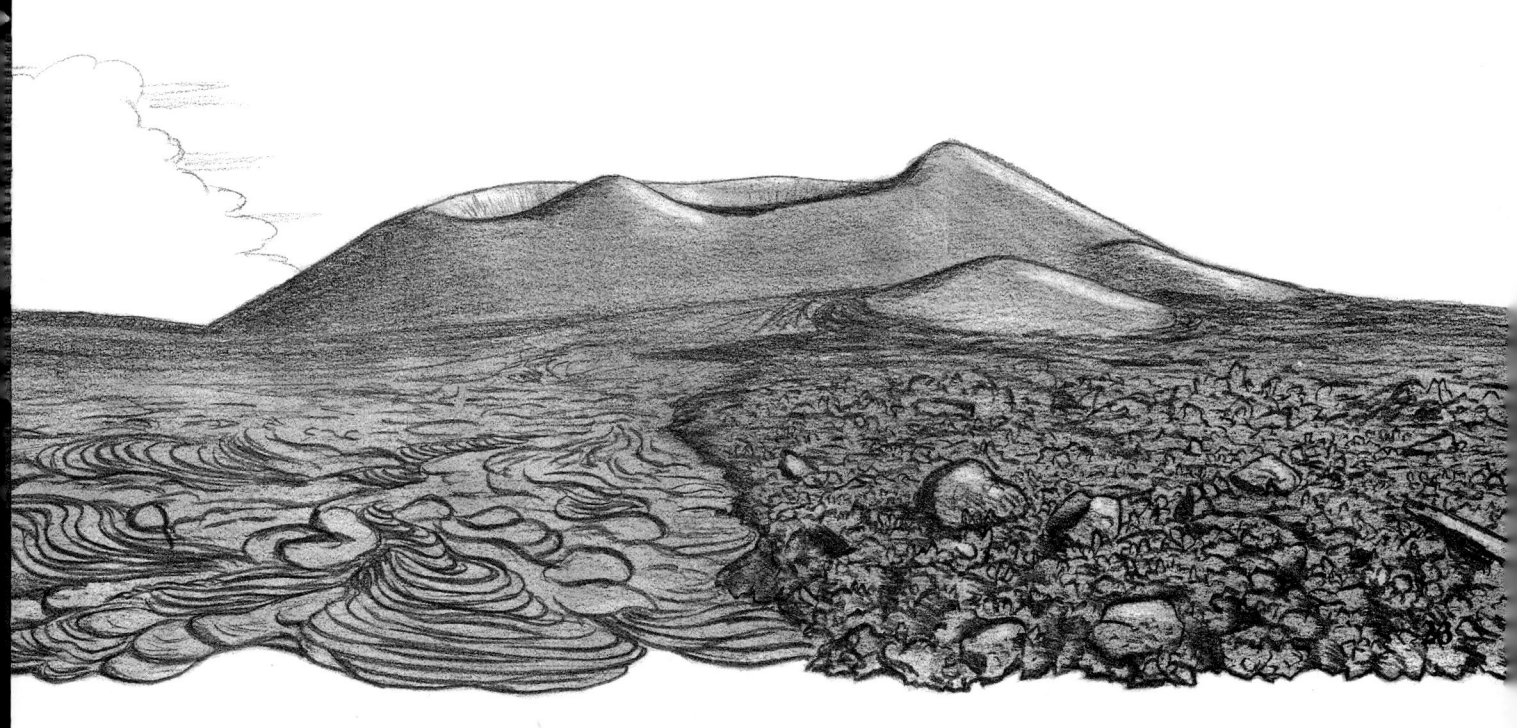

Mount Wellington broods over its lava fields a few years after the termination of its eruption, its explosion crater and the little mound of Purchas Hill just visible above the lava to the left. Unlike Mount Mangere, there was no final ash shower to cloak the lava flows which, as a result, lie exposed and bare, a hostile environment to plant or animal life for many years to come. Indeed, when Ferdinand von Hochstetter, the Austrian explorer and original cartographer of Auckland's volcanoes, saw Mount Wellington's flows about 130 years ago, they were still only partially covered in vegetation.

It sometimes happens that the same volcano produces both pahoehoe and aa flows; here, the pahoehoe flow occupies the centre of the picture and aa flows are either side. Today, these flows form the basis of the largest quarry in New Zealand. Both views look across what is now that quarry site from a point on College Road.

Rangitoto eruption

The Maoris on Motutapu, which was heavily populated at the time, must have thought the end of the world had come as great fountains of water, ash and steam were thrown up from an eruption centre only four kilometres from their island. Soon their island was to be deeply buried under a thick blanket of tuff and ash, smothering their settlements and gardens, and making Motutapu uninhabitable for a while.

The early stages of the eruption were probably exceptionally violent as cold sea water met molten rock. The sea was shallow, however, and within hours a broad explosion crater probably 100 metres or so deep had been excavated, within which fire fountaining soon began to build a number of cones.

Any other Auckland eruption would have been well into its allotted life span by now, but this one was different. Rangitoto's exact history is the subject of much debate, with some experts favouring a short but active life of about a decade approximately 600 years ago, while others argue for a more protracted history of intermittent eruptions commencing about 800 years ago and spanning about five centuries. However it was created, the result was a cone 259 metres high and a lava field that, in volume, equalled the output from all the previous Auckland volcanoes combined. Also unlike previous eruptions, that lava, at least towards the end, was not the liquid pahoehoe lava, but tended to be the more viscous aa.

When the volcano finally became extinct, lava that had saturated the base of the central cone cooled and shrank. The entire top of the mountain subsided by 10 to 20 metres as a result, leaving a moat-like ring round the summit, visible today as the irregular line of raised hillocks that seem to flank the cone from whatever angle it is viewed.

The volcanoes today

Only a few hundred years have passed since Rangitoto erupted yet in that time the Auckland area has experienced changes at least as profound as those of the previous 60,000 years. The arrival of European colonists and their decision to found a permanent settlement upon the isthmus — a settlement that has subsequently grown to be the largest city in New Zealand — has inevitably had a major impact upon the little volcanoes. Many were soon quarried away completely, their readily available supplies of rock being more than welcome to the builders of the new metropolis. Albert Park, so conveniently situated close to the heart of the expanding community, was among the first volcanoes to go, and several more soon followed. Others survived, but in a much mutilated state. Thus Mount Albert lost its summit, Three Kings is now a misnomer since only one remains, and others such as Puketutu, Maugataketake, McLaughlans and Pigeon Hill have been reduced to remnants of their former selves. Indeed, most of the cones have suffered to some extent from quarrying that continues even today.

Fortunately for the city, a number have survived to become public parks, standing like little green islands amidst the suburbs. Even where volcanoes have gone, the area has often been turned into a park or sports ground.

Best known of the surviving cones are One Tree Hill and Mount Eden, made popular both by their size and the fact that there is vehicular access to their summits. However, many of the other cones are open to the public, and several are well worth a visit by anyone curious about Auckland's volcanic past. In particular, Mount Mangere with its twin craters, the larger with a central tholoid, Mount Wellington with its awesome main crater, and Mount Richmond, with its huge explosion crater encircling a complex of little overlapping cones, repay exploration.

The explosion craters, like the cones, have suffered varied fates at the hands of humans. Several tidal lagoons or lakes now nestle amidst Auckland's more exclusive suburbs while, in sharp contrast, Mangere Lagoon now forms the sludge ponds of the sewage treatment plant.

And then there is Rangitoto, towering above its sister cones, visible from throughout Auckland, its familiar profile an integral part of the city itself. Too new and rugged to be an attractive site for colonisation by man, it has been left much to itself — a state of affairs that is likely to continue now it is part of the Hauraki Gulf Maritime Park. Limited quarrying has left small scars around the shoreline, and concrete pillboxes sprout amongst the jumbled basalt, legacies of the fortification of Auckland during the Second World War. The excellent road and track system was built largely by convict labour in 1930s and now helps make the island popular with day trippers.

The future

Will Rangitoto erupt again? It seems unlikely. Prolonged periods of quiescence have never been a feature of Auckland's volcanoes and, while the question of just how typical Rangitoto is of Auckland's volcanoes is still a subject for argument, it is generally felt that it has undergone its last eruption. On the other hand, there is nothing to suggest that this will be the last Auckland volcano.

Over the last 60,000 years, 48 volcanoes have

Auckland 250 years ago, shortly before the none-too-gentle hand of man, with his land reclamations and quarrying projects, changed things forever. The rising sea level has flooded several explosion craters and partly destroyed others. A number of low-lying lava flows have been submerged (dark grey). At the narrowest point, the waters of the Waitemata and Manukau all but meet, kept apart only by the bulk of Mount Richmond. Then, of course, there is the new addition, Rangitoto, rising from the bed of the old Waitemata River, dwarfing all previous volcanoes.

The addition of Rangitoto brings the total number of known Auckland volcanoes to 48. There may be a further cone buried beneath the lava flows of later eruptions, and the possibility that one or more small volcanoes lie beneath the waters of the Waitemata or Manukau Harbours cannot be totally discounted. All things considered, the Auckland volcanic field presents a record of fairly continuous activity that cannot be ignored.

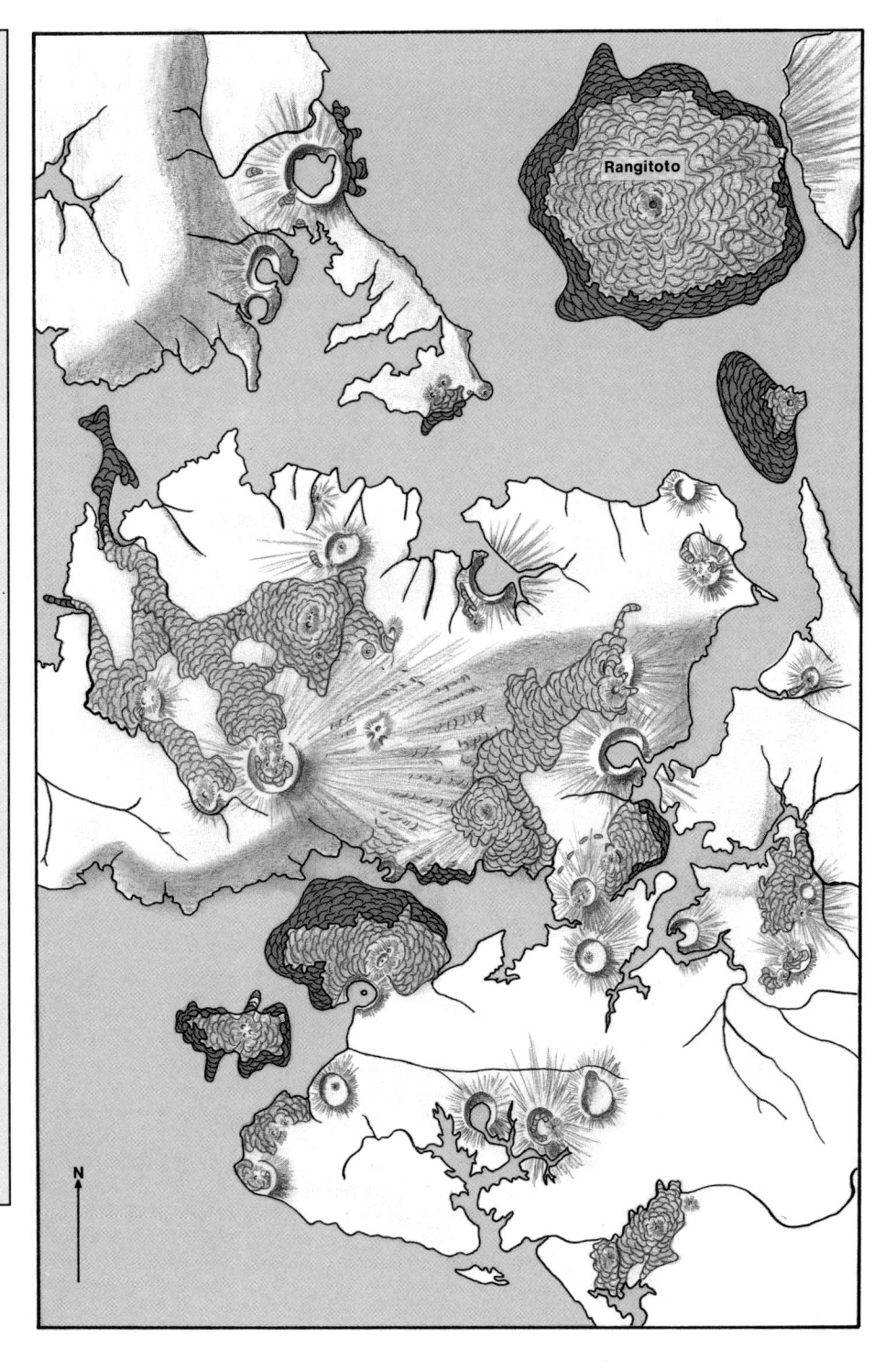

erupted in Auckland — an average of just under one every 1,000 years. But we know about 8,000 years separated the eruption of Rangitoto from the previous eruption at Mount Wellington, while on the other hand One Tree Hill and Mount Mangere erupted within a few centuries of each other; some volcanoes may even have erupted simultaneously.

In other words, we have no idea what will happen next. There is no reason why the arrival of the Europeans should have coincided with the end of volcanic activity. At any time, a new bubble of magma may break away from the hot spot and begin its rise to the surface. We will probably receive little warning of its coming — just a few earth tremors, most so minor that only seismographs will detect them, in the preceeding few hours or (if we are lucky) days. But when this will occur, or where, is anyone's guess.

The Remaining VOLCANOES of AUCKLAND

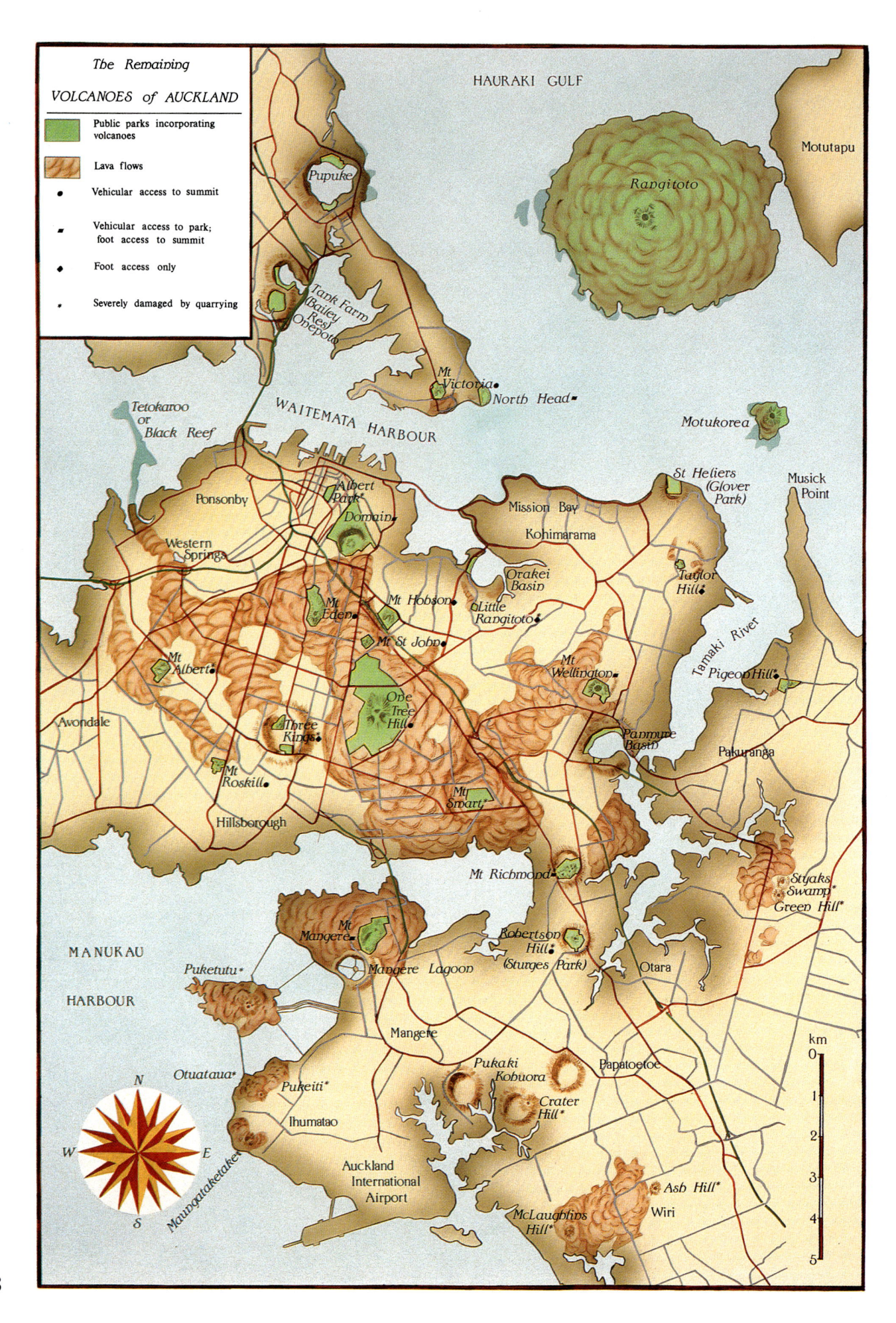

- ▨ Public parks incorporating volcanoes
- ▨ Lava flows
- • Vehicular access to summit
- ▬ Vehicular access to park; foot access to summit
- ◆ Foot access only
- * Severely damaged by quarrying

HAURAKI GULF

Motutapu

Rangitoto

Pupuke

Tetokaroo or Black Reef

Tank Farm (Bailey Rest) Onepoto

WAITEMATA HARBOUR

Mt Victoria • North Head ▬

Motukorea

Ponsonby

Albert Park*

Domain ▬

Mission Bay

Kohimarama

St Heliers (Glover Park)

Musick Point

Western Springs

Mt Eden • Mt Hobson •

Orakei Basin

Little Rangitoto ◆

Taylor Hill •

Mt Albert •

Mt St John •

Mt Wellington •

Tamaki River

Pigeon Hill •

Avondale

Three Kings •

One Tree Hill •

Panmure Basin

Pakuranga

Mt Roskill •

Hillsborough

Mt Smart *

Mt Richmond ▬

Styaks Swamp* Green Hill*

MANUKAU HARBOUR

Puketutu*

Mt Mangere

Mangere Lagoon

Robertson Hill • (Sturges Park)

Otara

Otuataua*

Pukeiti*

Ihumatao

Mangere

Pukaki Kohuora

Papatoetoe

Crater Hill*

Maungataketake*

Auckland International Airport

Asb Hill*

McLaughlins Hill*

Wiri

N W E S

km
0
1
2
3
4
5

28